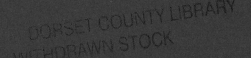

I'M GOOD AT
SCIENCE
WHAT JOB CAN I GET?

Richard Spilsbury

WAYLAND

First published in 2011 by Wayland
Copyright Wayland 2011

Wayland
Hachette Children's Books
338 Euston Road
London NW1 3BH

Wayland Australia
Level 17/207 Kent Street,
Sydney, NSW 2000

Commissioning editor: Camilla Lloyd
Project editor: Kelly Davis
Designer: Tim Mayer/Clare Nicholas
Picture research: Richard Spilsbury/Alice Harman
Proofreader and indexer: Alice Harman

Produced for Wayland by
White-Thomson Publishing Ltd
www.wtpub.co.uk
+44 (0)843 2087 460

British Library Cataloguing in Publication Data

Spilsbury, Richard, 1963-
I'm good at – what job can I get?.
Science.
1. Science–Vocational guidance–Juvenile
literature.
I. Title
502.3-dc22

ISBN: 9780750265751

Printed in China

Wayland is a division of Hachette Children's Books, an Hachette UK company
www.hachette.co.uk

Picture credits

1, Dreamstime/Melis82; 3, Dreamstime/
Igabriela; 4, Dreamstime/Mrloz; 5, Dreamstime/
Mikephotos; 6, Dreamstime/Yuri_arcur; 7,
Dreamstime/Baloncici; 8, Dreamstime/Leeser;
9, Dreamstime/Catman73; 10, Dreamstime/
Zebrik; 11, Dreamstime/Sivanagk; 12,
Dreamstime/Monkeybusinessimages; 13,
Dreamstime/Lampochka; 14, Dreamstime/
Eugene78, 15, Dreamstime/Mike_kiev; 16,
Dreamstime/Monkeybusinessimages; 17,
Dreamstime/Melis82; 18, Dreamstime/
Aleksandra Nadeina; 19, Dreamstime/Lisafx;
20, Dreamstime/Monkeybusinessimages; 21,
Dreamstime/Rixie; 22 Dreamstime/P3cpl;
23, Shutterstock/Oleksandr; 24, Dreamstime/
Igabriela; 25, Dreamstime/Radekdrewek; 26,
Dreamstime/Michaeljung; 27, Dreamstime/
Grosremy; 28, Dreamstime/Fotosmurf02;
29, Dreamstime/Showface; cover (top
left), Dreamstime/Mrloz; cover (top right),
Dreamstime/Mikephotos; cover (bottom),
Wikimedia/US Navy.

Disclaimer

CONTENTS

The world of science

What were *your* first scientific discoveries? Perhaps that water freezes into ice or that tadpoles change into frogs? Scientists observe and study natural phenomena and try to figure out patterns or rules to explain how they work. They study everything, from rivers and hailstones to people and planets.

The importance of science

Science has enabled people to make sense of the world around them. For example, scientists have discovered that the building blocks of all matter are different atoms. They have explored not just the Earth but also other parts of the universe, and they have identified the living things on our planet.

Scientists have used their knowledge of the natural world to help breed farm animals and grow crops and to create life-saving vaccines. Scientific discoveries have produced many vital technological developments, ranging from electricity and plastic to computers and submarines. Science has transformed life for many people, but the downsides of scientific progress are problems including global warming and pollution, which new scientific discoveries in the future may help us overcome.

Do you have the curiosity, patience and observation skills needed for a career in science?

Science in the workplace

Science is not just for scientists! Workers in many industries use scientific skills all the time. For example, mechanics use science to mend faulty engines and tennis players use science to hit a ball so it swerves through the air. Chefs use science to process, boil, freeze, grill, fry and bake ingredients into perfect food. Pharmacists use science to measure out and combine chemicals into drugs that comfort or cure patients.

Special skills

Scientists use a special technique called 'the scientific method'. First, they have an idea or hypothesis, then they carry out an experiment to see if the hypothesis is correct, record the results, and come to a conclusion based on the results. People who are good at science are generally curious about how things work or why things happen. They quickly build up special skills on their own and through study at school and college. Their scientific skills can be used in many different jobs – keep reading to find out about some of them!

← The work of scientists has enabled astronauts to explore and live in space.

PROFESSIONAL VIEWPOINT
'The scientist is not a person who gives the right answers, he's the one who asks the right questions.'
Claude Lévi-Strauss

Doctor

Doctors have important jobs in healthcare. They use their detailed knowledge of how the human body works to improve people's health or quality of life, cure disease, and ease suffering. Doctors are sometimes called medics or physicians.

Job description

Doctors:

- examine patients
- make diagnoses of illnesses and health conditions
- recommend and monitor treatment and give advice on health matters
- may train as GPs, surgeons or as specialists in different medical fields
- constantly improve their skills and keep up to date with medical advances
- when senior, may become registrars who manage other doctors.

↑ A doctor's job involves making medical decisions that can dramatically affect people's lives.

Different types of doctor

Some doctors work in general practice as GPs. They care for a number of patients with a wide variety of problems or issues, in a particular local area. Other doctors work in hospitals. Some hospital doctors work in accident and emergency departments, dealing with anything from cuts to car crash injuries. Other hospital doctors may be specialists. Surgeons carry out operations on particular body parts such as the spine or the heart. Anaesthetists use drugs to make people unconscious during operations.

Oncologists treat cancer and pathologists diagnose disease from tissue samples. Some doctors work as researchers in medical departments of universities or drug companies, and some in prisons. In the UK, most doctors work for the public National Health Service, but in other countries most doctors work in private practice, which means that they run their own businesses.

What skills do I need?

Doctors are high achievers at school, especially in sciences. It is very difficult to get into medical school, and you need to pass special tests and have voluntary work experience in healthcare-related settings such as clinics or hospices. Once accepted by a medical school, it takes a minimum of 10 years of training to become a qualified doctor. Successful doctors have to be good at communicating with patients, and also have excellent academic ability and an interest in health issues. Important skills include being caring, compassionate and sensitive about people's problems, and being able to put them at ease.

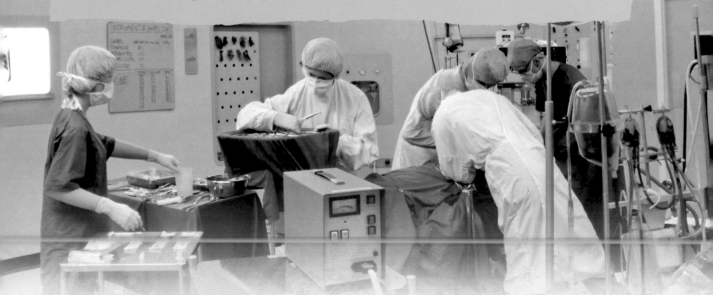

↑ Successful surgery depends not only on the practical skills and knowledge of surgeons, but also on the work of the rest of the surgical team.

Astronomer

Are you fascinated by the planets, how stars form, and the enormity of the universe? If so, you might like to become an astronomer. Astronomers study space, planets, moons, stars, comets and all the other components of our universe. They question how the universe began, when it might end, what it is made of and whether there is life out there – apart from on our planet!

Astronomers use (and sometimes create) different items of equipment to learn more about parts of the universe. These include giant optical telescopes to see and identify objects, and radio telescopes. These are special aerials that detect faint energy signals, which can help astronomers study the most distant parts of space. Some astronomical data and images come from special cameras and other sensors aboard spacecraft. Astronomers often test their hypotheses about the universe by comparing expected data with the data actually gathered.

Astronomers study distant marvels of the universe such as nebulas, which are enormous clouds of dust and gases where stars are born or die.

Job description

Astronomers:
- ask and answer questions about the universe
- collect and analyse data about space using mathematical calculations and computer programs
- write scientific papers about their results and present findings to different audiences
- design and operate technology used for gathering data about, or observing, parts of the universe
- may become university professors in astronomy, teaching students.

What skills do I need?

Astronomers regularly use physics, mathematics and IT skills to analyse images and complex data about the universe. They generally have a university degree in physics or astrophysics, and often a doctorate too. However, you have a head start if you are an enthusiastic stargazer and want to build up your astronomical skills.

Astronomers usually work in universities or at large observatories with other astronomers. Sometimes they travel to different observatories around the world to get the best views of objects in the universe. Astronomers may work closely with astronauts at times, but very rarely go into space themselves.

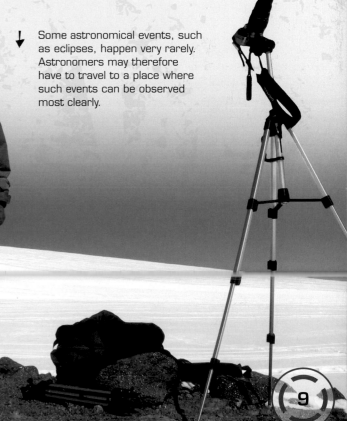

↓ Some astronomical events, such as eclipses, happen very rarely. Astronomers may therefore have to travel to a place where such events can be observed most clearly.

Biochemist

What are the substances inside plants that make them grow, or inside animals' brains that make them feel or remember? These are the sorts of questions that biochemists ask. Biochemists study the chemistry of living things. In particular, they study the chemicals that cells, tissues and organs produce during essential life processes, ranging from growth to reproduction.

— Job description —

Biochemists

• identify and analyse biological processes and problems, and develop techniques to investigate them
• design and conduct experiments, and make observations
• write up reports and present the results to others
• may work in protected environments on hazardous substances or on micro-organisms that can cause infectious diseases.

← A well-equipped laboratory is the usual work setting for a biochemist.

PROFESSIONAL VIEWPOINT

'Never be afraid to test something. You can't prejudge what a result is going to be for a particular experiment before you've done that experiment.'

Margit, biochemist

Different types of biochemist

Biochemists work in many different industries. Agricultural biochemists work on biochemicals that are important to farmers, for example by developing crops that are resistant to pest damage. Biochemists working in the food industry may develop food flavourings or check food safety in factories. Those in the pharmaceutical industry develop and produce medicines using biochemicals.

Clinical biochemists in hospitals test blood, urine and other body fluids, and their findings can help doctors make diagnoses. Some biochemists are called biotechnologists. They study, isolate and grow micro-organisms that make biochemicals which are useful for people. For example, they may find bacteria that help clear up oil pollution from water, or extract useful metals from soil, or make fuel from waste. Whatever industry they work in, biochemists spend a lot of their time in laboratories finding, studying and testing different chemicals.

↑ Some biochemists ensure that medicines such as antibiotics, which they create in labs, are carefully prepared in bulk quantities in pharmaceutical factories.

What skills do I need?

Biochemists need patience – they often have to sit or stand at a bench and use equipment for long periods of time. They also need to be accurate in recording their results and show attention to detail because they may have to repeat complicated procedures many times to get data. Some people work as technicians in biochemical laboratories with GCSE qualifications in science and maths. However, most biochemists have a biochemistry or chemistry degree.

Nurse

Are you caring, practical and unlikely to faint at the sight of blood? Then you might like to become a nurse! Nurses work with patients who are ill or injured, and their families or carers, giving support and advice, administering medicines and promoting good health.

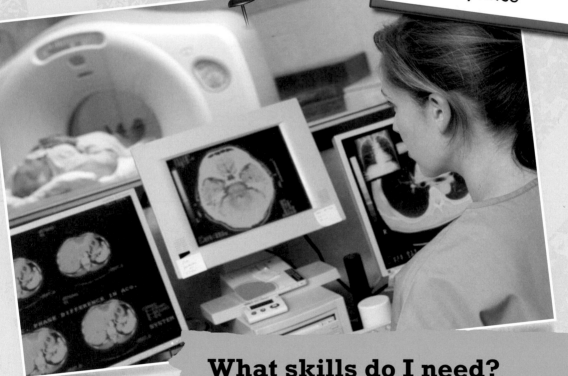

↑ This nurse has specialised training in using a CAT scanner, which is a device that produces images of the insides of patients to help medical diagnoses.

What skills do I need?

Good nurses are able to relate to other people. They remain calm and offer practical and emotional support, sometimes in traumatic or life-threatening situations. Nurses usually work as part of a team in a hospital or community setting. They need to stay focused, as they sometimes have long shifts and may need to work overnight.

Different types of nurse

There are four general types of nurse, working with different categories of patient. Adult nurses work with patients older than 18 years, and children's nurses care for anyone from sick babies to teenagers with cancer. Mental health nurses help people with mental health problems such as Alzheimer's disease, and learning disability nurses help those who struggle to learn (for example, because they have suffered brain injuries).

Nurses work in different places. Many work in hospitals and some specialise in particular departments. For example, neonatal nurses care for newborn babies, and triage nurses in an accident and emergency unit decide which patients' injuries need the most urgent attention from doctors. Other nurses work in health centres, schools or residential centres for older people. Some are district nurses who visit patients in their own homes and coordinate care from different specialists. Nursing skills are highly transferable so nurses can work in different countries, either in paid jobs or as volunteers, for example in response teams after natural disasters.

Neonatal nurses are experts in providing the medical care that vulnerable small babies need to stay alive.

Job description

Nurses:
- check and record changes in patients' health over time, for example by testing their blood pressure or temperature
- treat wounds and infections
- administer medicines prescribed by doctors
- carry out vaccinations
- make and monitor care plans for individuals
- may become senior nurses or sisters responsible for a team of nurses.

Geologist

Are you fascinated by fossils, gemstones or volcanoes? Then you might like to be a geologist. Geologists are scientists who study the Earth. They investigate its structure and types of rocks and how it has changed over time – for example, through erosion (wearing away) of rock. They also locate natural resources that are useful to people, ranging from metals through to oil and gas.

Different types of geologist

There are many types of geologist. Palaeontologists study the remains of organisms that lived in the distant past, such as fossilised bones of dinosaurs or shells. Geophysicists measure and interpret vibrations, movements or other changes in the Earth that may indicate past or future earthquake or volcanic activity. Hydrologists study and locate underground reservoirs of freshwater.

← Geologists carry out fieldwork to locate particular types of rock that may be of interest as clues in piecing together the history of the Earth.

Geologists:

- locate and obtain rock and soil samples in the field
- test samples in laboratories, for example by hardness or other properties
- may survey the geology of whole areas
- can use special technology to study rock deep underground
- may advise on extraction of geological resources
- when senior, may lead teams of geologists on projects.

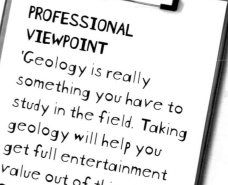

The work of geologists is vital for oil companies wanting to know exactly where to drill into the Earth to find oil supplies.

Geologists work in different settings. Some work mostly in laboratories, analysing rock samples, while others work mostly in the field. Fieldwork takes place worldwide, from remote mountains or deserts to urban settings, and is very variable. For example, geologists might locate new sources of valuable minerals such as diamonds, or test the firmness and depth of soil or rock to help engineers decide where to build large buildings.

PROFESSIONAL VIEWPOINT

'Geology is really something you have to study in the field. Taking geology will help you get full entertainment value out of this planet.'

Steve, geologist

What skills do I need?

Geologists need practical skills, such as using hammers or drills to obtain rock or soil samples, or using microscopes and chemical testing equipment in the laboratory. They also need to monitor and find evidence for gradual changes to the Earth over very long timescales. This requires good observation, patience and detective skills. Technicians in geological laboratories require GCSE qualifications, but professional geologists usually have degrees, for example in geology or geophysics.

Meteorologist

People often talk about the weather because it has a big impact on their lives. Would you like to be a weather expert for a living? Meteorologists observe, monitor and explain weather conditions. They forecast or predict future weather based on past trends and current data, and issue warnings about extreme weather and possible natural disasters such as floods or droughts. Meteorologists also monitor global warming – the general rise in temperatures worldwide – and its effects on changing weather patterns. Most scientists believe global warming is caused by gases, released when people burn fuels and trap the sun's heat in the atmosphere.

Job description

Meteorologists:

- collect data on air pressure, temperature, humidity, and wind speed and direction, on the ground and from sensors in the atmosphere
- process the data and interpret the findings, often using powerful computers
- present weather forecasts and meteorological data to different audiences, ranging from other scientists to TV viewers.

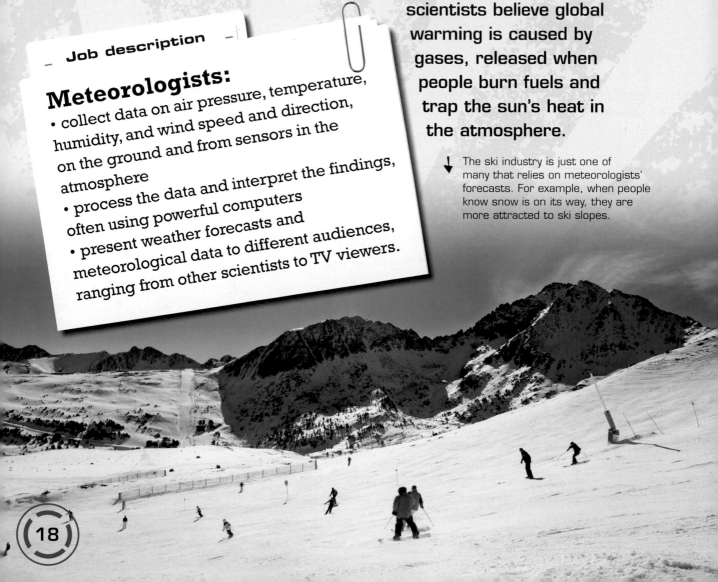

↓ The ski industry is just one of many that relies on meteorologists' forecasts. For example, when people know snow is on its way, they are more attracted to ski slopes.

Different types of meteorologist

Some meteorologists are forecasters who supply specialist forecasts for different industries. For example, some work for energy suppliers to help them plan when they will need to supply more power for heating in colder weather or air conditioning in warmer weather. Other meteorologists are researchers. They study detailed air flow, cloud and precipitation data to understand why weather changes. Their work is vital for forecasters trying to make more accurate predictions.

Most meteorologists work in the government Meteorological Office, in universities and in private forecasting companies. They often work closely with other scientists. These include oceanographers, who are specialists in how ocean temperatures and currents affect weather.

What skills do I need?

To be a meteorologist, it really helps to study maths and IT so that you can analyse complex weather data from many different sources. You should also study geography to understand weather and its formation worldwide. Meteorologists need patience, concentration and creativity to draw conclusions about weather trends from data.

PROFESSIONAL VIEWPOINT
'One of the most important things we do, and it is our mission, is to issue severe weather warnings, to protect life and property.'
Jeff, meteorologist

↑ Meteorologists use computers to help calculate future changes in weather, based partly on observation data.

Physiotherapist

↑ Some physiotherapists improve the mobility of their patients by carrying out exercises in swimming pools, because the water helps to support their bodies.

Job description

Physiotherapists:

- assess the needs of patients and provide treatments
- create and supervise exercise programmes
- use a wide range of therapies, ranging from massage and manipulation to ultrasound and laser treatments
- may start off as assistants and progress to become senior or consultant physiotherapists, leading teams.

The job of a physiotherapist is to help injured or ill patients become mobile, gain the ability to get around independently, and live more fulfilling lives. Physiotherapists work with patients of different ages with different mobility issues, mostly treating soft tissues such as muscles, or bones and joints. For example, they may move older people's limbs to improve their joint flexibility, massage sports players with muscle injuries, improve breathing for people with severe asthma, or help people who have damaged their legs in accidents to balance and walk again.

20

What skills do I need?

Physiotherapists need to be interested in people's health and well-being, and in human anatomy. To become an assistant physiotherapist requires science or health studies at A-level or BTEC standard, but to become a practising physiotherapist usually requires a university degree in physiotherapy or sports science. You can take this full-time or part-time while working as an assistant, which also provides valuable career experience. Remember that physiotherapists need to be good at putting people at ease in order to carry out their therapies. They also need to be happy with hands-on contact with patients.

Different types of physiotherapist

Physiotherapists work in many different places, from clinics and health centres to patients' homes. They may specialise in particular work, such as treating back pain or people recovering from surgery. Sports physiotherapists diagnose and treat sports injuries, and neurological physiotherapists help people who have problems with their nervous system such as a broken spinal cord. Physiotherapists may work full-time for one organisation or be self-employed.

Sports physiotherapists rapidly assess and treat injuries during rugby and football matches, to keep players on the pitch where possible or to take them off to avoid more serious damage.

PROFESSIONAL VIEWPOINT

'I love working with elite athletes who are focused and motivated. One of the best things I did to find out if I would enjoy this job was to shadow a physiotherapist for a day. Then I knew for sure!'

Tracy, sports physiotherapist

Dentist

The main job of a dentist is to monitor and improve the condition of a patient's teeth, gums and mouth. They do this through regular check-ups. Dentists look out for signs of tooth and gum disease through surface visual examination, and also by using X-rays to see inside teeth. They treat teeth, for example by drilling out decayed parts and filling the cavities. Dentists also advise patients on how to care for their teeth and offer cosmetic treatments that improve the visual appearance of teeth – for example, braces to straighten teeth and treatments to whiten them.

PROFESSIONAL VIEWPOINT

'What is special about dentistry is the high frequency of contact. You may see the same patient several times in one year. I enjoy helping people feel better about themselves by improving their oral health.'

Jung Lee, dentist

Job description

Dentists:
- inspect teeth, gums and mouths
- advise patients about oral health
- assess and inform patients about treatment options and plans
- fill or extract teeth
- make and fit crowns or braces, and carry out cosmetic teeth treatments
- may recruit, train and manage staff.

Dentists need to examine patients' mouths thoroughly in order to check their dental health, but they also have to work quickly in order to see all the patients on their list.

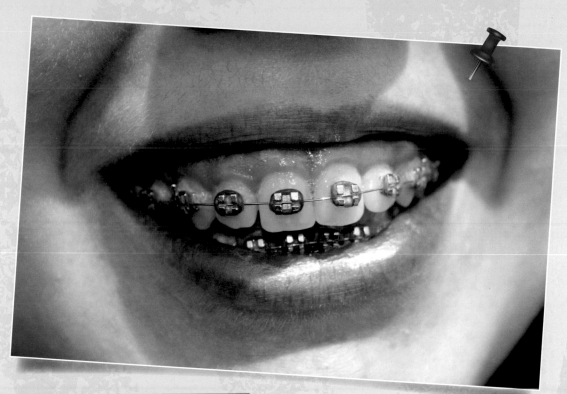

Different types of dentist

Most dentists look after a number of patients who are registered with their practice. Some dentists deal with more complicated or specialised treatment, and many of these work in hospitals. For example, dental surgeons carry out oral operations, orthodontists correct the positioning of teeth in the mouth, and peridontists treat serious gum diseases. Dentists generally work in practices as part of a team of dental care practitioners. This may include other dentists, dental nurses who assist the dentists during treatments, and hygienists who specialise in cleaning teeth and oral health.

↑ Orthodontists may make a brace or other dental aid to fit a particular patient's mouth.

What skills do I need?

To be a dentist, you will need to get excellent science A-level grades and then usually study for five years at a university dental school. Practical skills are useful, for example when drilling teeth, and it is vital to be able to make decisions under pressure and as part of a team. It is really helpful if you can put people at ease – remember that many people are frightened of going to the dentist!

Biologist

If you are interested in biology and the natural world around us, maybe being a biologist is the job for you. Biologists are people who study different aspects of living things, such as their diet, habitat, anatomy or behaviour. Biologists work in different places, from universities, zoos and conservation organisations to pharmaceutical, food and farming industries. They may divide their work between desk, laboratory and field (outdoor) study.

↑ This entomologist is collecting insects in the field for further study back in the laboratory.

Job description

Biologists:

• study living things in the environment and in the laboratory
• collect samples, carry out experiments, make observations and take measurements
• analyse results of experiments
• classify organisms
• provide specialist advice to organisations, for example about controlling pests or protecting endangered species.

Different types of biologist

Biology covers a wide range of subject areas, so there are many different types of biologist. Entomologists study insects, such as farm pests or honeybees. Marine biologists study ocean organisms, and they can usually scuba dive. They may study fish populations for government quotas, or study damage to marine life after an oil spill. Microbiologists study tiny living things such as bacteria, for example how they cause food to go off or cause illnesses. Ecologists study the relationships between organisms and their environment.

What skills do I need?

All biologists need to have enquiring minds and be good at problem-solving and analysing information and data. Most biologists have a university degree, and sometimes a postgraduate qualification. Most biologists also do voluntary work or paid placements during school and university holidays, to gain valuable experience before applying for a job. Many also join biological societies or clubs to keep up to date with developments and discoveries, and try to get experience of a wide range of living things, from keeping pets and growing plants to studying animals in the wild.

Some zoologists work closely with captive animals in zoos, for example cleaning out and feeding penguins. →

PROFESSIONAL VIEWPOINT
'Science is a subject that involves far more communication and cooperation skills than most people realise. If you are a difficult person, you had better learn to get along with your peers and supervisors.'
Jeffrey, marine biologist

Dietitian

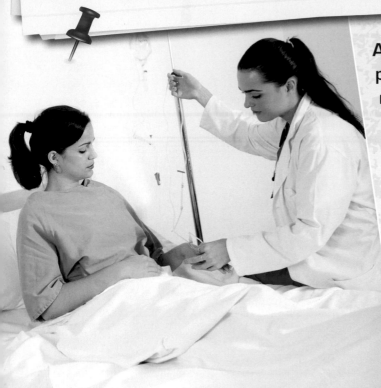

A dietitian provides people with practical advice about nutrition requirements, specialist diets, and the links between food and health. They work with individuals and groups of people, helping them to make healthy food choices for their situation, for example if they are ill or want to lose weight. Many dietitians work in hospitals, or in industries including sports, food and research.

← Dietitians sometimes recommend that patients have a drip. Liquid food goes through a tube into a vein to give nutrition to people who can't eat or absorb food normally.

PROFESSIONAL VIEWPOINT

'Giving really practical advice to athletes about food and fluid choices, as well as explaining the science, is a key element in success. Helping them achieve their sporting goals through good nutritional practices is an exciting and rewarding career.'

Lucy, sports dietitian

Job description

Dietitians:

• study a person's current diet to see whether it is linked to any health issues
• work out a diet based on the patient's wants and needs
• explain complex issues about nutrition to the patient
• keep up to date with scientific research and government guidelines about diet
• teach health professionals, such as doctors and nurses, about diet issues.

Different types of dietitian

The National Health Service is a major employer and many dietitians work in hospitals, often in a specific department, such as with children or advising people who need a special diet because of their medical condition. Some dietitians work in sports organisations, helping athletes eat in a way that improves their performance. Some work in the food industry, advising food manufacturers on the nutritional content of their foods. Some dietitians work in universities, developing and testing foods. Some work for the government, making sure that consistent, accurate messages about nutrition are promoted through the media.

What skills do I need?

Dietitians need to be caring, good at communicating with and motivating people, and interested in science and nutrition. They also need a knowledge of chemistry for analysing foods. All dietitians must have a qualification approved by the Health Professions Council (HPC). Some dietitians take a university degree in dietetics, others take diplomas after a first degree in a science subject such as chemistry. As well as theory, dietitian courses include practical training in a hospital or community setting.

Dietitians can make a big difference to the performance of top athletes by recommending the right nutritional regime.

Forensic scientist

Forensic scientists are the people who find, collect and interpret samples or clues. Their scientific findings are used to support investigations by the police and other agencies into crimes and accidents.

At crime scenes, forensic scientists work closely with police officers in order to find samples without disturbing other possible evidence.

Forensic scientists work on three main types of samples. Chemical samples could include chemicals left over after fires, biological samples may be spots of blood left on a murder weapon or hair on a carpet, and drug samples include illegal drugs in urine or tissue samples. They analyse the samples using a range of techniques such as DNA profiling, microscope examination and chemical tests. The samples can be used, for example, as evidence, proving a person was present at the scene of a crime.

What skills do I need?

The most useful skills are probably chemical analysis and IT skills for processing samples. The work demands great patience and concentration, and you need an inquisitive, open mind to remain unbiased about what you are analysing. Most forensic scientists study chemistry or biochemistry and then start off as assistants on forensic teams. You cannot do this job if you get squeamish at the sight of blood or crime scenes!

Different types of forensic scientist

Most forensic scientists work for private forensic businesses on samples brought forward by police forces or private investigators. Some have particular specialisms. For example, forensic entomologists examine the different types and ages of insects such as maggots on dead bodies, because they give clues to how recently and where a person died. Forensic scientists work closely with police officers at the scene of a crime, and with pathologists who assess the medical significance of evidence.

Forensic scientists need only analyse a tiny sample of blood to find out who it came from.

PROFESSIONAL VIEWPOINT

'The work can be very time-consuming, but I still get a thrill from finding evidence that nobody expects to find, evidence that can completely change the course of an enquiry.'
Gareth, forensic scientist

Glossary

administer to give medicine or drugs

analyse to examine the structure or nature of something logically

atom tiny, invisible building block of matter

bacteria microscopic living things found in huge numbers in water, air and soil. Some cause disease and others are useful, for example to make yoghurt

brace metal device to help teeth grow straight

crop plant grown and harvested for food or other use

diagnosis identifying or discovering the cause of something, such as an illness

DNA profiling finding the pattern of DNA in a sample, usually in order to match it to the known pattern in an individual person

evidence facts, objects, signs or other clues that help confirm something is true

fossil transformed remains of ancient living things, such as dinosaur bones

global warming general increase in average world temperatures, caused by atmospheric pollution from power stations, vehicles, etc

healthcare services ranging from doctors to hospitals, which provide medical care

humanely with kindness and without suffering

hypothesis unproven theory, idea or method of explaining something

laboratory room or building used to carry out scientific experiments, tests or research

massage using hands to press and rub someone's body to relieve pain or increase mobility in joints or muscles

mental health emotional and psychological well-being, such as being able to interact with others or cope with stress

pharmacist person who prepares medicines for sale

phenomena facts or events that are not fully understood

pollution substances added to soil, air or water, making it dirty or harmful, such as an oil spill

sensor device that reacts to light, heat, movement or other stimuli, making a machine operate in a particular way. For example, motion sensors can turn a security light on

spinal cord major mass of nerves inside the spine, connecting the brain with nerves in the limbs and other body parts

sports science study of how sports performance is affected by internal factors such as nutrition, and external factors such as exercise

universe space and everything in it, from planets to stars

vaccine substance usually injected into the blood to protect someone against a disease

X-ray type of invisible energy wave that can pass through objects and be used to make an image of what is inside them

Further information

There are many specific courses, apprenticeships and jobs using science skills, so where do you go to find out more? It is really useful to meet up with careers advisers at school or college, and to attend careers fairs to see the range of opportunities. Remember that public libraries and newspapers are other important sources of information. The earlier you check out your options, the better prepared you will be to put your science skills to good use as you earn a living in future.

Books

All in a Day's Work: Careers Using Science, Megan Sullivan, National Science Teachers Association, 2006

Career Ideas for Kids Who Like Science (Career Ideas for Kids), Diane Lindsay Reeves, Facts On File Inc, 2007

Disease-hunting Scientist: Careers Hunting Deadly Diseases (Wild Science Careers), Edward Willett, Enslow, 2009

Robot Scientist (Cool Careers in Science), Kathleen Manatt, Cherry Lake, 2007

Science (Discovering Careers for Your Future) Infobase Publishing, Facts On File Inc, 2004

Sports (Discovering Careers for Your Future) Infobase Publishing, Facts On File Inc, 2005

Volcanologists (Cool Careers in Science), Kathleen Manatt, Cherry Lake, 2007

Websites

www.bls.gov/k12/science.htm
This site lets you explore possible careers of chemists and environmental scientists.

http://egsc.usgs.gov/isb/pubs/booklets/scientists
A website with lots of information about careers in natural sciences such as geology and biology.

www.futuremorph.org/11-14/home.cfm
An interesting and interactive site that could really help you sort out your future career in science. It includes 'My Future Finder', with links to jobs such as nuclear scientist, mining engineer and optician, the 'What might you be?' game, and 'Globe Plotter', which gives you an idea of the global impact of science.

www.prospects.ac.uk/industries_science_overview.htm
This website introduces you to the world of science careers, including links to some job roles. Although aimed at science graduates, it gives a clear idea of what routes to take for many different careers using science skills.

www.wetfeet.com/Careers-and-Industries/Careers/Science.aspx
A site that summarises science careers, and possible career paths. Go to the same URL and replace the word 'Science' with 'Medical and Health', 'Nursing' or 'Pharmaceuticals' to discover more about some other careers.

Index